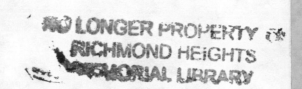

ANNE FRANK

YONA ZELDIS McDONOUGH • ILLUSTRATED BY MALCAH ZELDIS

HENRY HOLT AND COMPANY   NEW YORK

For my children, James and Kate
—Y. Z. M.

For Nancy F. Karlins, my friend,
whose dedication to art is an inspiration
—M. Z.

The author and illustrator would like to thank Alex Sagan
at the Center for European Studies, Harvard University,
for offering helpful comments on the manuscript and illustrations.

Henry Holt and Company, Inc., *Publishers since 1866*, 115 West 18th Street, New York, New York 10011

Henry Holt is a registered trademark of Henry Holt and Company, Inc.
Text copyright © 1997 by Yona Zeldis McDonough. Illustrations copyright © 1997 by Malcah Zeldis
All rights reserved.
Published in Canada by Fitzhenry & Whiteside Ltd., 195 Allstate Parkway, Markham, Ontario L3R 4T8.

Library of Congress Cataloging-in-Publication Data
McDonough, Yona Zeldis. Anne Frank / by Yona Zeldis McDonough; illustrated by Malcah Zeldis.
Summary: Traces the life of a Jewish girl who chronicled her day-to-day life
in a diary as she hid in an attic in Nazi-occupied Holland for two years.
1. Frank, Anne, 1929-1945—Juvenile literature. 2. Jewish children in the Holocaust—Netherlands—Amsterdam—
Biography—Juvenile literature. 3. Amsterdam (Netherlands)—Biography—Juvenile literature. [1. Frank, Anne, 1929-
1945. 2. Jews—Netherlands—Biography. 3. Holocaust, Jewish (1939-1945)—Netherlands—Amsterdam. 4. Women—
Biography.] I. Zeldis, Malcah, ill. II. Title.
DS135.N6F7349 1997 940.53'18'092—dc21 [B] 96-37677

ISBN 0-8050-4924-X / First Edition—1997
Printed in the United States of America on acid-free paper.
1 3 5 7 9 10 8 6 4 2
The artist used gouache on Strathmore watercolor paper
to create the illustrations for this book.

IMPORTANT DATES

JUNE 12, 1929   Anne Frank is born in
Frankfurt am Main, Germany.

FEBRUARY 1934   Anne moves to Amsterdam, Holland,
where she starts school.

SEPTEMBER 1939   Hitler's armies invade Poland and World War II begins.

JUNE 12, 1942   Anne receives a diary on her thirteenth birthday.
In it she writes to an imaginary friend called Kitty.

JULY 6, 1942   The Frank family moves to the secret annex.

JULY 13, 1942   The Van Pels family moves into
the annex with the Franks.

NOVEMBER 16, 1942   Fritz Pfeffer joins the group in the annex.

AUGUST 4, 1944   Anne and the others are arrested in their hideaway.

SEPTEMBER 1944   The prisoners are sent to Auschwitz,
a concentration camp in Poland.

OCTOBER 1944   Anne and Margot are moved to Bergen-Belsen,
a concentration camp in Germany.

FEBRUARY or
MARCH 1945   Anne and Margot die of typhus.

SUMMER 1947   Anne's diary is published in Dutch.
In 1952 the English edition,
Anne Frank: The Diary of a Young Girl, is published.

Early one rainy July morning, a young girl and her parents left home and walked swiftly through the quiet streets. Although it was hot, they were dressed in heavy winter clothes: the girl wore two undershirts, three pairs of underpants, a dress, a skirt, a jacket, shorts, two pairs of stockings, lace-up shoes, a woolly hat, a scarf, and still more. Other clothes and papers were stuffed into the bags they carried. The bags were heavy and the rain poured down, but no one offered a ride to the small group. The girl didn't know that it would be more than two years until she would walk outside again. Her name was Anne Frank.

Anne Frank was born in Germany. Her parents, Edith and Otto Frank, were German Jews. They came from the town of Frankfurt am Main, where Otto's family had lived for generations. First the Franks had a daughter named Margot. Then, on June 12, 1929, Anne was born. The Franks' house was in a pretty neighborhood where Anne played happily in her sandbox or with the many other children who lived nearby.

But outside the loving world of Papa, Mama, and Margot, bad things were happening in Germany. People lost their jobs and had no money for food and clothes. They were scared and angry. They wanted a leader who promised an end to their problems. Adolf Hitler, who came to power in 1933, seemed like such a leader. He told the Germans that they were better than all other people on Earth. He blamed Germany's troubles mainly on the Jews. He immediately began passing laws that discriminated against the Jews. Hitler and all the people who supported him were called Nazis, a shortened version of the German word *Nationalsozialist*, which means National Socialist.

Anne's father saw that it was not safe to be a Jew in Nazi Germany so when Anne was four, he took his family to Amsterdam, in the Netherlands. The Franks liked their new home. It was not far from the shore, and they spent happy summer holidays on the beach.

When Anne started school at the age of five, she quickly learned to read and write. She was a good student and had lots of friends. Because Anne was outgoing and lively, she often was given lead parts in the school plays.

In 1939 Hitler declared war on Poland. War broke out across Europe, and soon Hitler's armies reached the Netherlands, where Anne and her family lived.

Even with the war going on, Anne still had fun with her friends. History, movie stars, cats, and dogs were among her favorite things. Another favorite thing was the little red-and-white-checked diary she got from her parents as a thirteenth-birthday present. Anne was thrilled by the gift and thought of it as her best friend. She wanted to give it a name, so all the entries in the diary began with "Dear Kitty."

Writing to Kitty, Anne described how Hitler's anti-Jewish laws had spread to Holland. Slowly, Jews had lost their jobs and their possessions had been taken away. All Jews over the age of six had to wear a six-pointed yellow Star of David on their clothing. Although Anne did not know it, her father was making plans for the family to go into hiding.

In July 1942 the Frank family moved into a hidden apartment in the back of the building that housed Otto Frank's business. Anne called it the secret annex. The entrance to their rooms was blocked by a movable bookcase that was built just after they settled in. Only seven people knew that the family was there. Four of them worked in Otto's office. These friends smuggled food and clothing to the Franks when they could. Had they been caught by the Germans, they could have been put to death.

After the Franks had been living in the secret annex for about a week, they were joined by Mr. and Mrs. Van Pels and their fifteen-year-old son, Peter. Anne was glad that Peter had brought along his pet cat, Mouschi, since Anne had had to leave her own cat behind when they left home. In November the last member of their little group, a dentist named Fritz Pfeffer, came to stay as well.

RICHMOND HEIGHTS

Life in hiding was not easy for Anne. She was often bored and lonely. She longed for her friends, her school, and most of all her freedom. Living in such close quarters with near-strangers was not easy either. Many times, there were arguments. Anne quarreled with her mother and sister. She even felt misunderstood by her beloved father. All of her sadness and frustration were poured out into the pages of her diary, Kitty, who was her friend throughout.

Anne told Kitty how strange she felt during the first few days in the secret annex. She missed her friends, the black bicycle on which she rode to school, and the room in which she had grown up. Since the Franks were frightened of being discovered, they had to whisper and tiptoe around during the day. Only at night could they relax a little, although they still had to take care not to be seen through the windows. Using scraps of different materials, Anne and her father stitched together some curtains that they pinned to the walls.

Yet Anne was brave. She tried hard to stay busy and cheerful.
She spent time reading and doing schoolwork, so she wouldn't
be too far behind when she was finally able to return to school.
She worked on a detailed family tree of all the kings and queens
of Europe and she learned shorthand. She loved to look at
photos of her favorite movie stars and paste their pictures on
the walls of her bedroom. Even in hiding there were still little
treats and surprises, like the time when Anne, who was growing
quickly, outgrew her shoes and was given a pair of red high
heels by Miep Gies, one of the devoted friends who knew their
secret.

The attic was Anne's special place, since it had a small window that could be opened to let in a glimpse of the stars, sunshine, or the tower across the street. Anne and Margot often went up there to read. And when Anne and Peter formed a special friendship, the attic was the place where they got together to talk.

Alone in the attic, Anne often thought about the life she hoped to lead when the war ended. She wanted to be a writer. In addition to her diary, she wrote fairy tales and other imaginary stories. She even began work on a book called *Stories and Events from the Secret Annex*. And when she learned that the Dutch government hoped to publish all wartime diaries, she started to copy hers out neatly, on lined paper. She cherished the dream that someday her words would be read by people all over the world.

Although the little group was cut off from the rest of the world, they managed to hear news from a radio kept in Otto's office. At night, they would creep into the room and turn it on. When Anne heard that the Germans were losing the war, she felt hopeful. She wrote in her diary that, despite everything, she still believed that people were really good at heart.

But someone discovered the Franks' hiding place and told the police. On August 4, 1944, the secret annex was raided by German and Dutch Nazis. Anne and the others were now prisoners. The Franks, the Van Pels, and Fritz Pfeffer were sent to Westerbork, a concentration camp in Holland, where they were made to work for the Nazis.

A month later, they were sent to Auschwitz, a concentration camp in Poland. The conditions there were terrible. Anne, Margot, and their mother were forced to work with little food, water, or clothing. Many people around them died of hunger and sickness. Many others were killed outright by the Nazis. In October the two girls were sent to Bergen-Belsen, a camp in Germany. Their parents were left at Auschwitz, where their mother, Edith, died in the infirmary. It was a long, cold winter and the girls got sick. First Margot died of typhus and a short while later Anne died too. She had not yet turned sixteen.

Anne's diary and other papers were found in the annex by
Miep Gies, who kept them. After the war ended, Anne's father
went back to Amsterdam. He was the only one from the secret
annex who survived the hard winter at Auschwitz. When he read
the diary Miep gave him, he decided it should be published.

Anne's little book became extremely popular and it was
translated into many languages. Because people were amazed
by Anne's courage and maturity, the story of her life was
made into a play and the building where she and her family hid
was turned into a museum. Anne Frank lives on through her
remarkable words, which are an inspiration to millions of people
all over the world.

AUTHOR'S NOTE

Initially, a modest 1,500 copies of Anne Frank's diary were published in 1947. French and German translations appeared soon afterward. The first English edition, *Anne Frank: The Diary of a Young Girl*, was published in 1952. Since then, the diary has been published in more than fifty languages. At least twenty-five million copies have been sold worldwide. Perhaps with the hope of its eventual publication in mind, Anne chose to use false names for the Van Pels family, Fritz Pfeffer, and their Dutch friends. Those are the names that appear in the published diary. In this book, however, I have decided to use the real names of those involved, which at this point are well known.

Although the precise number of Jewish victims is hard to establish, many scholars of the period agree that approximately six million Jews died at the hands of the Nazis. Nor were Jews their only victims: Romanies (Gypsies), Slavs, Communists, homosexuals, the mentally or physically handicapped, and anyone else whom the Nazis considered to be subhuman were all singled out for imprisonment, slave labor, and death.

While many of the concentration camps were built to exploit the slave labor of Jews and others, the Nazis also constructed special extermination camps whose main function was to kill—chiefly by gassing—the vast majority of those sent to them. The purpose of these camps was to be a secret, and most, like Auschwitz where Anne and her family were sent, were in isolated areas of Poland. Since Margot and Anne spent only a short time at Auschwitz before being transferred to Bergen-Belsen, it is likely that their Nazi captors thought them young and strong enough to continue working.

Before writing a biography of Anne Frank for young children, I asked myself, What is the point of telling this story to young children? Wouldn't it be better to shield them from its horrors, at least for a little while longer? Is this a story that I would want my own children to hear? Finally, I came to believe that there is value in the telling, even—or perhaps especially—to those who are young. War, racism, and death may not be easy for children (or anyone else) to understand. Nevertheless, we are sometimes called upon to explain the inexplicable. It is my hope that this book might be helpful to those introducing the Holocaust to children.

—Y. Z. M.